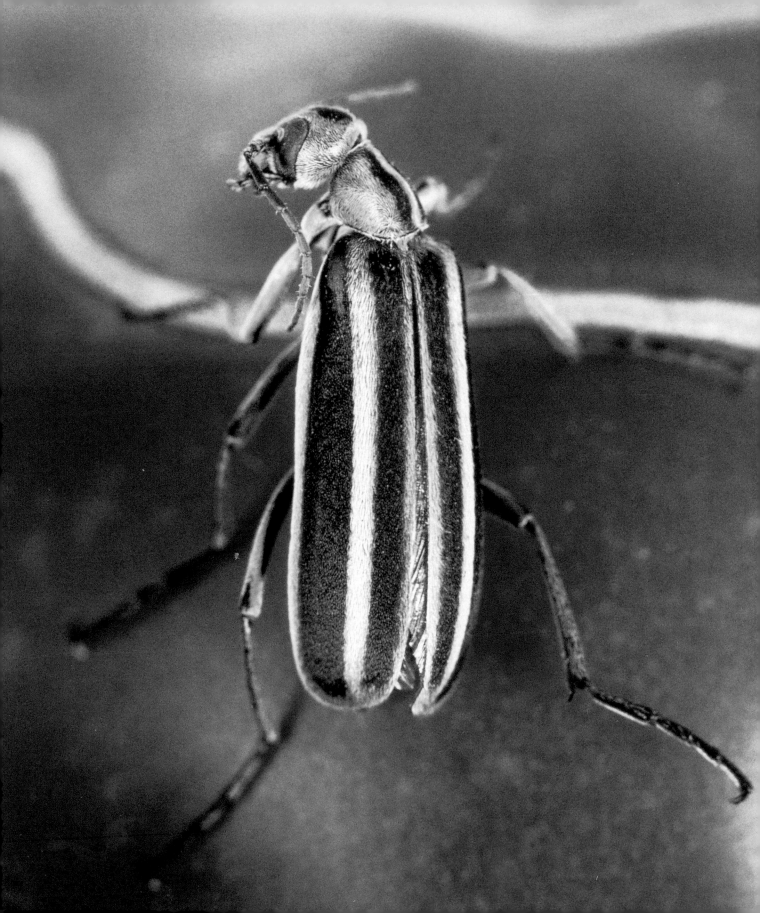

LIFE VIEWS

Published by Creative Education
123 South Broad Street, Mankato, Minnesota 56001
Creative Education is an imprint of The Creative Company

Art direction by Rita Marshall; Production design by The Design Lab/Kathy Petelinsek

Photographs by David Liebman

Library of Congress Cataloging-in-Publication Data
Halfmann, Janet. Life in a garden / by Janet Halfmann p. cm. — (LifeViews) Includes index
Summary: Examines several animals that may thrive in a garden, including aphids,
praying mantises, and garden snails. Suggests several related activities.
ISBN 1-58341-072-4
1. Garden animals—Juvenile literature. 2. Garden ecology—Juvenile literature. 3. Gardening.
[1. Garden animals. 2. Garden ecology. 3. Ecology.] I. Title. II. Series: LifeViews (Mankato, Minn.)
QL49.H28   1999
591.75'54—dc21   99-10293

First Edition

2 4 6 8 9 7 5 3 1

LIFE IN A
GARDEN

JANET HALFMANN

PHOTOGRAPHS BY DAVID LIEBMAN

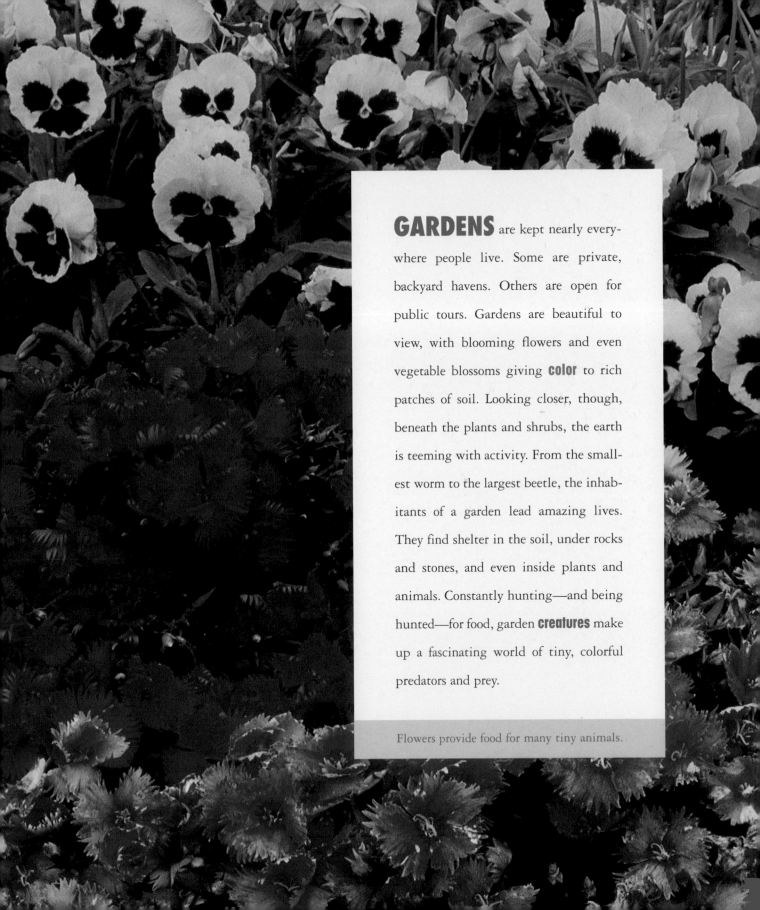

GARDENS are kept nearly everywhere people live. Some are private, backyard havens. Others are open for public tours. Gardens are beautiful to view, with blooming flowers and even vegetable blossoms giving **color** to rich patches of soil. Looking closer, though, beneath the plants and shrubs, the earth is teeming with activity. From the smallest worm to the largest beetle, the inhabitants of a garden lead amazing lives. They find shelter in the soil, under rocks and stones, and even inside plants and animals. Constantly hunting—and being hunted—for food, garden **creatures** make up a fascinating world of tiny, colorful predators and prey.

Flowers provide food for many tiny animals.

Nematodes are everywhere in the garden. These worm-like creatures, usually too small to be seen without a microscope, are also known as roundworms or eelworms. Nematode means "threadlike," and that's just what these wrigglers look like: living bits of white thread. A nematode doesn't have eyes or a brain. Its body is covered with a tough **skin** filled with pockets. These pockets are sensitive, letting the nematode know what's going on around it. Scientists know of about 30,000 species, or kinds, of nematodes. However, it is believed that close to half a million species haven't yet been discovered.

Some nematodes have teeth, which they use when hunting tiny animals and other nematodes. Others consume bacteria, algae, and fungi. Root-knot nematodes have a hollow spear called a **stylet**. They use it like a straw to sip plant juices. Nematodes that are parasites live inside caterpillars and other insects. They lay eggs inside the insect. The larvae that hatch eat their insect home.

Meat-eating fungi are the main predators, or hunters, of nematodes. Fungi nab them with rings or trap them with

More than 100,000 species of butterflies and moths are known. As caterpillars they go through metamorphosis, changing into winged insects. The smallest moth has a wingspan of 0.2 inches (5 mm); the largest butterfly, 11.8 inches (30 cm).

sticky knobs and nets. **Marigolds** are flowers that are poisonous to nematodes. Some kinds of nematodes, such as the hookworm and pinworm, cause diseases in animals and humans.

Insects are often much larger than nematodes. Vining plants, such as cucumbers and pumpkins, attract the **spotted cucumber beetle**. As soon as the tiny plants push through the ground in spring, the beetles are on them. These bright yellowish-green beetles are about the size of a bean and have 11 or 12 spots on their wings. The head, legs, and antennae are black. They belong to a large group called **leaf beetles**. Spring brings the adults out from their snug winter hiding spots under leaves and trash near the garden. Some beetles migrate from warmer places. The adults feed on the roots and leaves of young vine plants.

For the tiny **aphid**, the garden is like a candy shop. This pinhead-sized insect has a giant appetite for sugary juice. It consumes sap from plants through a long hollow tube, or proboscis. The aphid's soft body looks like a **teardrop**. The 4,000 species of aphids come in many colors. Green, black, and white are the most common, but some are red, pink, orange, or

Beetles are one of the most common of all insect varieties. More than 25,000 kinds of leaf-eating beetles exist, including the striped blister beetle (above) and the caterpillar hunter (opposite). The Japanese beetle is a garden pest.

brown. Common aphids in the garden are the pale-green pea aphid and the powdery-looking, green-gray cabbage aphid.

Where there are aphids, there are bound to be other insects with a sweet tooth—especially ants. That's because aphid bodies produce a sweet substance called **honeydew** made from the sap that they don't need. Ants like this sticky liquid so much that they often tend a "herd" of aphids, much like a farmer with cows.

Because they're surrounded by enemies such as syrphid flies, lacewings, and ladybugs, aphids must produce many offspring to keep their species alive. Despite the larger size of their predators, the tiny aphids fight back. Two tubes on the end of the abdomen give off an alarm odor called a **pheromone**. It irritates an attacker's mouth and also warns other aphids of danger.

A major enemy of aphids is the **ladybug**, also known as the ladybird beetle. The ladybug is a fierce hunter, devouring about 8,000 aphids in its lifetime. Ladybug young also feast on aphids. When a mother ladybug lays her clusters of yellow-orange eggs in spring or early summer, she puts them close to

Chemical insecticides are used to control insect pests, but they also kill good insects. Organic gardeners—those who do not use chemicals—rely on insect predators such as ladybugs, praying mantises, and certain types of wasps to control damaging bugs.

an aphid colony. The miniature eggs hatch into black **larvae** with orange splotches. They waste no time scrambling over leaves on their six legs hunting for aphids. They pierce the aphids with their hollow jaws and draw out the juices. The young eat for two to three weeks and then attach themselves upside down under leaves to form pupae. In about a week, the adult ladybugs emerge.

Ladybugs are one of the best-known garden helpers. All but a handful of the 5,000 species are insect predators. Besides aphids, they feed on mites, mealy bugs, rootworms, scale insects, and thrips. Unlike many other predators, ladybugs won't leave the garden if they run ′out of insect prey to eat. They'll switch to **nectar** and **pollen**, with favorites being tansy, angelica, and scented geraniums.

Ladybugs look like tiny pea-sized domes with spots. The familiar convergent lady beetle is orange or red with twelve black spots. Other kinds are black, yellow, or gray and have from 2 to 24 spots, or no spots at all. Like all beetles, ladybugs have four wings. The hard outer wings form the ladybug's

Brightly colored spiders, looking like flowers, attract insect prey.

colorful shell and protect the flying wings underneath. Ladybugs have six legs with tiny claws at the end, two
eyes, and two short antennae.

Before winter comes, hundreds—or sometimes
thousands—of ladybugs gather together to find a place to keep
warm. Under rocks, tree bark, or dead leaves, they sleep for the
winter, living on the fat stored in their bodies. This behavior is
called **hibernation**. When spring comes, each ladybug awakens
and goes its own way to hunt for aphids and search for a mate.

The ladybug is also in danger of being eaten by predators.
One defense is its bright red shell, which is a signal that warns
enemies of the ladybug's **poison**. When threatened, the ladybug
squirts a smelly, bad-tasting liquid from its leg joints. If this
doesn't work, the ladybug may lie on its back and pretend to
be dead. Despite its best defenses, though, the ladybug often
falls prey to the garden spider.

The **garden spider** is a major predator of garden insects. All
of the 30,000 species of spiders in the world have fangs, and
most of them contain poison. Only a few kinds are harmful to

The crab spider can change color to blend in with its surroundings. Unlike many
spiders, it does not build a sticky web to catch prey; rather, it waits until an unsus-
pecting fly or beetle comes close, then pounces on the insect and kills it.

people. Many people think the spider is an insect, but it belongs to a group called arachnids. Insects have six legs and three body sections, but arachnids have eight legs and two body parts. A spider's eight legs are jointed and have claws at the ends to help it cling to webs. Although most spiders have eight eyes, not all species—including the garden spider—can see well. A spider has fingerlike organs called **spinnerets** at the rear of its abdomen. These are used for spinning silk. Liquid silk flows through hundreds of tiny nozzles on the spinnerets and dries into strong thread. All spiders spin silk, and most build webs.

Garden spiders make beautiful lacy webs. Most of the larger webs are made by females. Garden spiders belong to a group called **orb weavers**. Their webs look like orbs, or circles. An orb weaver begins its web by sticking one end of a single thread to a twig or plant and letting the other end flutter in the wind until it sticks to something. The spider then finishes the web's frame and adds spokes, like a bicycle wheel. Next, it spins a spiral of sticky threads, which becomes a trap for prey.

A beautiful common orb weaver is the black-and-yellow

No two species of orb weaver spiders makes the same form of web; each of their patterns is distinct. Usually, only the center of the web is sticky, and most insects are caught by chance. Some webs, however, reflect sunlight to lure insects.

garden spider. Bright yellow and black patterns decorate its body and legs. The female's body is about as big as a large jelly-bean, and males are smaller.

In the fall, male and female garden spiders mate. The female wraps her eggs—about 1,000 of them—in a silk case and attaches it to a plant stem. The case is about the size of a marble. Baby spiders, called **spiderlings**, hatch from the eggs, but they spend the winter inside the case. Since they are meat-eaters like their parents, the babies eat one another. In spring, the remaining spiderlings chew their way out of the case. This four-stage process—egg, larva, pupa, and adult—is called **metamorphosis**.

Another garden predator sits perfectly still on a plant in the garden with its large front legs raised. With big, bulging eyes that stare from its triangle-shaped head, it keeps a sharp lookout for prey. This is the **praying mantis**, the only insect on earth that can swivel its head and look over its shoulder. When it spots an insect, it shoots out its spiny front legs as quick as lightning to grab it. Then it bites the prey to paralyze it.

The wasp (above), though it can attack and sting humans if provoked, is a beneficial insect. It can destroy many harmful insect pests. The wasp is just one of the insects a praying mantis (opposite) will eat.

The praying mantis isn't fussy about what it eats and snatches anything it can get its front legs on—aphids, bees, beetles, butterflies, caterpillars, and even toads and small birds.

Victims rarely see the mantis before it strikes. Although mantises are fairly large—as long as a little finger—their green or brown color blends in with the garden plants. This is called **camouflage**. Of the 1,700 species of mantises in the world, only a few kinds live in North America. The most common is the European praying mantis.

Adult mantises don't have many insect enemies because they're such fearless hunters. Bigger animals, such as birds and lizards, prey on them. Mantises avoid danger by flying away or by appearing fierce. Predators may think twice when a mantis spreads its wings and rears up on its hind legs.

Other creatures come out only at night. These include snails and slugs. Both are plant-eaters and need damp, cool places so their bodies won't get dry. The 80,000 species of snails and slugs belong to an animal group called **mollusks**.

Plants and animals depend on each other for survival in a garden. Foam egg sacs and webs are built on plants. Many spiders and insects pollinate fruit and flower plants.

This group also includes clams and octopuses. All mollusks have soft bodies and a special structure called a mantle. The mantle produces the snail's spiral shell, adding coil after coil as the snail grows. The slug has a raised mantle on its back instead of a shell.

Snails and slugs are known as **Gastropods**, which means "stomach footed." They get their name from the flat jelly-like foot that runs along the bottom of their bodies. They glide along on this foot, which pours out slime. This slime track makes movement easier and protects the foot on rough surfaces. Snails and slugs leave a silvery trail of **slime** wherever they go.

Garden snails and slugs feel for food with four tentacles that wave from the head. The longer pair has eyes at the tips for telling light from dark. All of the feelers can be pulled inside the head to protect them.

Just below the feelers is a tiny mouth, and inside is an amazing tongue. It's covered with thousands of tiny sharp **teeth**. The long tongue rubs on leaves, scraping off bits of food. They eat just about any kind of plant, living or dead, and can

Most snail shells coil to the right, and their internal organs are looped throughout the shell. While land snails and slugs are related to saltwater sea snails and slugs, salt can be deadly to land species and is often used to control their numbers in fields and gardens.

actually be quite damaging to flowers and crops. Tiny new plants are especially at risk.

One of the most common slugs in the garden is the gray garden slug. It is smaller than a paper clip and varies in color from cream to gray, with brown splotching. Each slug lays up to 100 round jelly-like **eggs** underneath boards, dead leaves, or flowerpots—anywhere the soil is moist. In the warmth of spring and summer, the babies hatch in about 10 days. They look like the adults, but smaller.

Snails and slugs don't like the hot, dry days of summer or the freezing cold of winter. They often come out on rainy, cloudy days. In winter, both snails and slugs burrow into the ground and hibernate, living off their fat until spring.

For many **creatures**, from the invisible nematodes to the larger snails, the garden is a vast world of its own. For most people, public or private gardens are nearby and easy to explore. Every garden is filled with wondrous creatures, each fulfilling its special role in the web of life.

Gardens are home to many large, winged insects.

PRAYING MANTIS PETS

You can watch these fascinating insects up close by hatching young from an egg case and raising them in a small cage.

Home

A mantis home should be large enough for the insect to move around. A one-gallon glass jar or aquarium works well. Cover the top of the cage with screening material to give your mantis air. Add a small, living branch or stem with leaves for climbing. Put the cage in a lighted location, but never in direct sunlight.

The Egg Case

One way to watch mantises hatch and grow is to find an egg case on a branch. Cut the branch several inches below the case. If you can't find an egg case in the wild, you can order one from a nature supply company or even from some gardening catalogs. (Mantises are often used by farmers to control pesky insects.) Get a species that lives wild in your area, or you will not be able to release the new mantises outside. If it's cold when you get the egg case, keep it in the refrigerator until spring, when you'll be able to find enough insects for the babies. It takes only one to three weeks for the babies to emerge from the egg case once it is warmed up to room temperature.

Hatching Babies

If you purchased an egg case, you must gently tie it to a branch. Put the branch and egg case in a cage as described above. Put another branch containing aphids into the cage as well, if possible. Mist the egg case and cage occasionally, but do it lightly. When the babies hatch, keep a few to raise and release the rest outdoors where they can find insects to eat in the wild.

Caring for Mantises

For about a month, feed the babies aphids or other small insects such as fruit flies. Later, they can be fed crickets and flies. If they don't get enough food, the young mantises will eat one another, so be sure to feed them plenty of insects. Put water in a shallow jar lid inside the cage. Don't use too much water, as baby mantises can drown easily. You'll want to release the mantises as they grow up and get wings. Adult mantises prefer to live alone, so keep only one in a cage. Remove the jar lid and replace it with a shallow cup of water to keep the aphid branches alive. You'll need to replace these branches often. If you can't catch enough live insects for your mantis, live crickets can be purchased from a pet store. Gently mist the container once a week to provide water for the mantis.

PLANT A GARDEN

It's fun to plant a garden. Choose seeds that grow in your area. Some easy-to-grow vegetables that you can start from seed are beans, peas, corn, cucumbers, lettuce, pumpkins, zucchini, and radishes. Marigolds, zinnias, sunflowers, and nasturtiums are easy flowers to grow. Follow the package directions for the best time of year to plant them, then watch your garden—and its critters—grow.

Use a shovel to turn the soil. The soil should be dry and flaky. If it's too wet when you dig, the soil will form hard clods that plants can't push through.

Break the turned soil into smaller pieces with the shovel or a hoe, then rake the soil smooth.

Use a trowel, hoe, or your fingers to make a trench for the seeds. Read the directions on the seed package to find out how far apart and how deep to plant the seeds. Keep the seed packets so that later, after the garden sprouts, you can read the packets to find out how much to thin the plants.

Label each row with a marker.

LEARN MORE ABOUT GARDENS

National Gardening Association
180 Flynn Avenue
Burlington, VT 05401
http://www2.garden.org/nga/
    LOBBY/home.html

Young Entomologists' Society, Inc.
6907 West Grand River Avenue
Lansing, MI 48906-9131
E-mail: YESbugs@aol.com
http://members.aol.com/YESbugs/
    mainmenu.html

Royal Botanical Gardens
680 Plains Road West
Hamilton/Burlington, ON
Canada L7T 4H4
http://www.rbg.ca/

The Evergreen Foundation
355 Adelaide Street West, Suite 5A
Toronto, ON
Canada M5V 1S2
E-mail: info@evergreen.ca

The New York Botanical Garden
200th St. & Kazimiroff (Southern) Blvd.
Bronx, NY 10458-5126
http://www.nybg.org/

Center for Insect Science
Education Outreach
Life Sciences South, Room 225
The University of Arizona
P.O. Box 210106
Tucson, Arizona 85721-0106
E-mail: insected@u.arizona.edu
http://insected.arizona.edu

Missouri Botanical Garden
4344 Shaw Blvd.
St. Louis, MO 63110
E-mail: freeland@mobot.org
http://www.mobot.org/welcome.html

INDEX

All life in a garden is somehow connected.